CW00751430

DEPARTMENTAL LOCOMOTIVES, UNITS AND COACHING STOCK

Rich Mackin

AMBERLEY

First published 2017

Amberley Publishing
The Hill, Stroud
Gloucestershire, GL5 4EP

www.amberley-books.com

Copyright © Rich Mackin, 2017

The right of Rich Mackin to be identified as
the Author of this work has been asserted in
accordance with the Copyright, Designs and
Patents Act 1988.

ISBN 978 1 4456 7126 0 (print)
ISBN 978 1 4456 7127 7 (ebook)

All rights reserved. No part of this book may be
reprinted or reproduced or utilised in any form
or by any electronic, mechanical or other means,
now known or hereafter invented, including
photocopying and recording, or in any information
storage or retrieval system, without the permission
in writing from the Publishers.

British Library Cataloguing in Publication Data.
A catalogue record for this book is available from
the British Library.

Origination by Amberley Publishing.
Printed in the UK.

Foreword

For almost as long as there have been railways, there has been 'departmental' rolling stock. This name is used to describe any vehicle that plays a part in the running of the railways without carrying passengers or goods. Ranging from engineer's vehicles, to generator vans, to vehicles used to help move specific types of stock on the network, these unsung heroes play a pivotal role in the running of the UK's railway network. Some are purpose-built but the majority are converted, usually from redundant passenger stock.

While the use of departmental coaches, multiple units and locomotives has dwindled in recent years due to changes in railway operations, there is still a wide variety of unusual vehicles in use all over the network. This book aims to point the spotlight at these vehicles, covering those that currently work on the railway, along with a look at now-withdrawn departmental stock and former departmental vehicles that have entered preservation or reverted to their original intended roles.

While many types of departmental vehicles have all but disappeared from the current railway scene, such as engineer's coaches, infrastructure operator Network Rail still maintains a large fleet of infrastructure testing and monitoring trains, operated on their behalf by Colas Rail Freight, and this book highlights these in particular. Other operators, such as Direct Rail Services and Chiltern Railways, either use or have recently used departmental stock of their own, and this book covers some of these vehicles too.

No. 1256, Darlington, 23 August 2014

In recent years, the departmental coaching stock number series has largely been discontinued, with converted vehicles retaining their previous identities. Mk 2F No. 1256, previously a First Open with a buffet at one end used by Virgin CrossCountry, has been converted into a Plain Line Pattern Recognition coach. It is seen at Darlington on 23 August 2014.

No. 5981, Darlington, 20 April 2013

With large numbers of later Mk 2 coaches leaving passenger service in the early 2000s, Network Rail took the opportunity to acquire a number of vehicles for departmental service. No. 5981, a Mk 2F Standard Open previously used by Virgin CrossCountry, has become a Plain Line Pattern Recognition coach. It was captured in a test train formation at Darlington on 20 April 2013.

No. 5981, Darlington, 12 July 2014

No. 5981 is seen at Darlington again, on 12 July 2014, this time being conveyed in an unusual formation powered by two Class 43s.

No. 6262, Darlington, 4 March 2016

Generator van No. 6262, converted from Mk 1 brake No. 81064/92028/92928, has had two of the wide doors on either side removed when it was seen at Darlington on 4 March 2016.

No. 6264, Darlington, 24 July 2006

Network Rail own a number of generator coaches, converted from Mk 1 gangwayed brake coaches. Still retaining the original wide doors and most of the windows from its previous career, No. 6264 (formerly No. 80971, then No. 92023, then No. 92923) is in a test train formation at Darlington on 24 July 2006.

No. 6263, Preston-le-Skerne, 2 June 2015

Tucked in behind a Direct Rail Services Class 37, generator van No. 6263 passes Preston-le-Skerne (near Aycliffe on the East Coast Main Line) on 2 June 2015.

No. 6263, Darlington, 30 May 2016

During an overhaul, the Mk 1 generator vans had two of the four wide doors on either side removed. No. 6263 shows the revised bodyside arrangement at Darlington on 30 May 2016.

No. 9481, Darlington, 4 March 2016

Mk 2D Brake Standard Open has been acquired by Network Rail for use as a support coach. Previously in use with First Great Western as a seated coach on the Night Riviera sleeper service, it received a large disabled toilet while the gangway connection at the brake end was removed. It is seen passing Darlington on 4 March 2016.

No. 9481, Newcastle, 27 March 2017
Support coach No. 9481 is later seen in the formation of a test train passing Newcastle on 27 March 2017.

No. 9516, York, 27 March 2016
A later Mk 2F Brake Standard Open, No. 9516, has been acquired by Network Rail for use as a break force runner. Formerly in service with Virgin CrossCountry, the only modifications made to the vehicle have been the removal of the large-width doors at the brake end of the coach. The original seating is visible in the passenger saloon as the coach leaves York on 27 March 2016.

No. 9523, Darlington, 4 March 2016

Also in use as a brake force runner, Mk 2F No. 9523 (formerly a Brake Standard Open) has had even fewer alterations than No. 9516, still retaining the brake area doors. It is seen passing Darlington on 4 March 2016. Prior to departmental service, it was also in use with Virgin CrossCountry.

No. 9523, Preston-le-Skerne, 2 June 2015

Brake force runner No. 9523 is seen in a test train formation at Preston-le-Skerne, near Aycliffe, on 2 June 2015.

No. 9701, Darlington, 23 August 2014

British Rail converted a total of fourteen Mk 2F Brake Standard Opens into driving vehicles for Class 47s in Scotland. Classified as Driving Brake Standard Opens, the DBSOs worked in Scotland, then East Anglia until they were eventually replaced by Mk 3B vehicles. Now known as Remote Train Operating Vehicles (RTOVs), No. 9701 is one of five such coaches acquired by Network Rail after withdrawal from passenger service. Fitted with a generator and seating/kitchen/shower, they allow test trains to be operated by one locomotive while providing extra amenities for staff.

No. 9702, Darlington, 30 May 2016

Remote Train Operating Vehicle No. 9702 brings up the rear of an Ultrasonic Test Unit formation at Darlington on 30 May 2016. Preserved No. 37025 was leading at the other end.

No. 9703, Doncaster, 13 November 2008

Mk 2F RTOV leads a test train into Doncaster West Yard on 13 November 2008. This was one of the first vehicles to return to use with Network Rail, reducing the need to hire in additional locomotives for 'top and tail' working.

No. 9708, Norwich, 22 March 2013

Mk 2F Remote Train Operating Vehicle No. 9708 has received some alterations to work with the Structure Gauging Train – it has been fitted with a bar coupling at one end, to allow adequate space between it and Optical Gauging Car No. 460000. The redundant corridor connection has also been removed. It was found that Network Rail's new yellow livery interfered with the train's own structural gauge readings, reflecting enough light to produce incorrect data! The inner ends of the adjacent vehicles were soon painted black, as seen at Norwich on 22 March 2013.

No. 9708, Derby, 13 September 2014

As part of the Structure Gauging Train, Remote Train Operating Vehicle No. 9708 has been fitted with an array of forward-facing lights. It is seen at the head of the new formation (SGT2) at Derby on 13 September 2014. The roof-mounted exhaust vent for the generator can also be seen above the former brake area. By this time, the inner black end has been removed, and the corridor connection refitted.

No. 9714, Darlington, 27 May 2013

RTOV No. 9714 brings up the rear of a formation at Darlington on 27 May 2013. The ventilation grille for the generator can be seen behind the cab door, the equipment fitted in the former brake area.

No. 9714, Doncaster, 28 March 2013

Mk 2F RTOV No. 9714 enjoys the sun at Doncaster West Yard, 28 March 2013. The plated-over window is a sign of the internal modifications made to the vehicle, designed to provide a wash/rest area for test train crews.

No. 82124, Derby, 13 September 2014

Network Rail own a number of Mk 3B Driving Van Trailers, cascaded from passenger duties in the mid-2000s. The DVTs underwent a number of modifications, including an onboard generator and a forward-facing camera. Intended to work with Class 67s, the DVTs saw use when DB Schenker operated test trains with such locomotives. Network Rail provided No. 82124 as an exhibit during an open day at Derby Etches Park, where it is seen on 13 September 2014.

No. 72612, Darlington, 7 September 2013

In the early/mid-2000s, Network Rail acquired a number of Class 488 trailer sets, displaced from Gatwick Express by new Class 460 EMUs. The former Mk 2F coaches were initially used as brake force runners before being converted for infrastructure testing. No. 72612, former Mk 2F Standard Open No. 6156, became part of Class 488 set No. 8307 in 1984, working between London Victoria and Gatwick Airport for twenty years. Acquired by Network Rail in 2004, it was part of brake force runner set No. 910002 before becoming a Radio Survey Train coach. It is seen here at Darlington on 7 September 2013.

No. 72616, York, 27 March 2016

Radio Survey Train coach No. 72616 leaves York behind No. 68004 on 27 March 2016. Originally built as Mk 2F Standard Open No. 6007, it joined the Gatwick Express fleet in 1984, converted into a Class 488. As with other Class 488 vehicles, it was acquired by Network Rail after withdrawal from passenger service. After a period in brake force runner set No. 910001, No. 72616 was converted into a Radio Survey Train coach.

No. 72630, Darlington, 17 July 2014

Acting as a support coach for the current Structure Gauging Train, No. 72630 was previously a Gatwick Express coach (originally Mk 2F Standard Open No. 6094).

No. 72631, Newcastle, 27 March 2017

Former Gatwick Express coach No. 72631 was converted into a Plain Line Pattern Recognition coach in 2012. The 'PLPR' vehicles record a continuous video of the track beneath with the capability to recognise defects such as damaged sleepers and missing clips. An operator reviews flagged images to verify the defect and schedule repairs. No. 72631 is 'PLPR1' and is seen at Newcastle on 27 March 2017.

No. 99666, Darlington, 17 July 2014

Originally built as Mk 2E First Open No. 3250, No. 99666 was converted into an exhibition coach in the 1990s, one of a number of such vehicles that could be hired by companies who used them on promotional tours around the country. When these trains came to an end, Network Rail acquired No. 99666 for use as a support coach. The windows were plated over and the interior was removed during its time as an exhibition coach, allowing the interior to then be fitted out to the customer's specifications. It is seen passing Darlington on 17 July 2014.

No. 975091, Darlington, 12 July 2014

With a career dating back to 1973, No. 975091 is an Overhead Line Monitoring Coach. Originally named *Mentor*, it is fitted with a pantograph for measuring the state of overhead wires. Lines are often measured at speed, necessitating 100 mph locomotives for which Colas Rail acquired a pair of Class 67s.

No. 975091, Newcastle, 27 March 2017

No. 975091's pantograph is raised as it approaches Newcastle – the train had worked from Heaton to Glasgow, and was working back to Derby. It returned home via the Durham coast, taking in Sunderland, Hartlepool, Stockton, Eaglescliffe and Northallerton.

No. 975091, York, 27 March 2016

No. 975091 leaves York in a 100 mph formation powered by Class 68s on 27 March 2016. No. 975091 often operates at this speed, which necessitated the provision of such locomotives – Colas Rail Freight now use their own Class 67s.

No. 975081, Norwich, 22 March 2013

Originally built as Mk 1 Brake Standard Corridor No. 35313, No. 975081 was originally Laboratory 17 *Hermes*. Undergoing a rebuild at one end it gained a Class 421/423-style cab. It later joined the Structure Gauging Train, eventually losing nearly all trace of the cab it gained. It is seen in Norwich on 22 March 2013, just weeks before withdrawal.

No. 460000, Norwich, 22 March 2013

No. DC460000 was a unique vehicle, built on a four-wheel steel wagon chassis as an optical gauging car for British Rail's Structure Gauging Train. Painted black so as not to reflect light, beams of light (later replaced by lasers) were projected outward from the centre of the vehicle and the time it was taken to reflect that light back was used to measure distances from lineside structures such as platform edges, bridges, tunnels and signals. No. DC460000 was withdrawn in the spring of 2013, replaced by a more compact system fitted to a Mk 2 coach. The unique optical gauging car was disposed of at the end of 2015. It is seen here at Norwich on 22 March 2013, shortly before withdrawal.

No. 975280, Norwich, 22 March 2013

Originally converted from Mk 1 Brake Composite Corridor No. 21263, No. 975280 was Laboratory 18 *Mercury*. Deployed on the West Coast Main Line, it was used to test the trackside transponder systems to be used in the Control-APT system for the Class 370 Advanced Passenger Train. After the APTs were withdrawn, it became part of the Structure Gauging Train, acting as a support coach. It is seen here as part of the Structure Gauging Train at Norwich on 22 March 2013.

No. 975280, Derby, 13 September 2014

In the spring of 2013, the Structure Gauging Train was withdrawn, being replaced by a modern set-up in a pair of Mk 2 coaches. Former support coach No. 975280 is seen in the sidings at Derby's RTC on 13 September 2014, stored among other vehicles. At the time of writing it remains at Derby.

No. 977985, Derby, 13 September 2014

Previously Mk 2F First Open No. 6019, then Gatwick Express coach No. 72715, No. 977985 forms part of the current Structure Gauging Train. The laser scanning equipment (used to measure the distance between the vehicle and any surrounding structures) is contained in a drum that extends from one end of the coach. It is joined to sister vehicle No. 977986 using a long bar coupling and is seen here at Derby on 13 September 2014.

No. 977986, Derby, 13 September 2014

After the original optical gauging car No. DC 460000 was withdrawn, it was replaced by No. 977986. Originally built as a Mk 2D First Open, No. 3189, then declassified and renumbered No. 6231, it became exhibition coach No. 99664 in the 1990s. Exhibition trains were used for travelling shows, either held by British Rail themselves or by companies who could hire, paint and fit out the vehicles to suit their needs. Exhibition trains declined throughout the late 1980s and 1990s, and after falling out of use No. 99664 was acquired by Network Rail and used as a brake force number before becoming No. 977986 and being used in the new Structure Gauging Train from 2013 onward.

Structure Gauging Train (SGT2), Derby, 13 September 2014

The 'drum' extending from No. 977985 is clearly visible as SGT2 awaits its next duty at Derby, 13 September 2014. This took the place of optical gauging car No. DC460000 the year before. Below the drum is the long bar coupling that semi-permanently couples this coach to No. 977986.

No. 31233 and SGT2, Derby, 13 September 2014

Network Rail's No. 31233 sits at the head of the new Structure Gauging Train (SGT2) at Derby on 13 September 2014, showing the additional spotlights fitted to the locomotive in the early 2000s. No. 31233 was the last of Network Rail's Class 31s to be withdrawn, with the veteran locomotive finally bowing out in April 2017.

No. 977868, Darlington, 2 April 2013

The first of several Radio Survey Coaches in Network Rail's fleet, No. 977868 was converted from Mk 2E Standard Open No. 5846. Converted in the mid-1990s, it is used to measure the reception on radio-based railway communication systems (NRN, then GSM-R).

No. 977969, Darlington, 2 April 2013

Prior to departmental service, No. 977969 was originally built as No. 14112, a Mk 2B Corridor Brake First, before entering service in the Royal Train as No. 2906, a generator/support vehicle, before seeing departmental use. It is seen at Darlington, in its current guise, on 2 April 2013.

No. 977969, Darlington, 22 May 2016

After working as part of the Royal Train for a number of years, No. 2906 entered departmental service in 2004 as a generator/support vehicle, providing power and accommodation for Network Rail staff employed on test trains. It is seen passing Darlington on 22 May 2016.

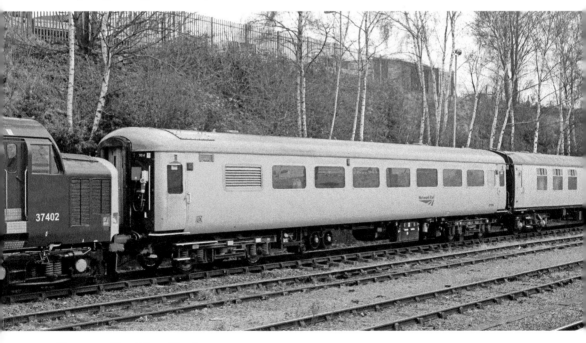

No. 977974, Norwich, 22 March 2013

Converted from Mk 2F Standard Open No. 5854, No. 977974 first saw departmental use as part of the original New Measurement Train (NMT) formation in May 2003. Due to a 'lively' ride at high speeds, it was later replaced by a converted Mk 3, before seeing use in Hitachi's battery-powered 'Hayabusa' experiment, then becoming a locomotive-hauled Track Inspection Coach (dubbed 'TIC2'). It often saw use in the old Structure Gauging Train formation, and was resting at Norwich on 22 March 2013. As TIC2 it replaced an older vehicle, No. 999508.

No. 977997, Darlington, 17 July 2014

Originally built as a Mk 2F Standard Open, No. 6126 became Class 488 trailer No. 72613 when it was modified for Gatwick Express use in 1984. After twenty years working between London Victoria and Gatwick Airport, it was acquired by Network Rail. After a time as a brake force runner it was converted into Radio Survey Coach No. 977997, dubbed 'RSC3'. Still bearing the high-level Southern Region multiple working cables at the nearest end, it works in locomotive-hauled test trains.

No. 977997, Newcastle, 27 March 2017

The other side of No. 977997 shows heavier modifications, with more plated-over windows and one replaced with a ventilation grille. It is seen pausing at Newcastle on 27 March 2017.

No. 977997, Darlington, 7 September 2013

The external modifications to Radio Survey Coach No. 977997 are evident as it passes Darlington on 7 September 2013.

No. 999508, Darlington, 6 July 2008

No. 999508 was purpose-built as an inspection saloon, one of a small batch built by British Rail at Swindon in 1960. It was converted into a track inspection coach in 1987 and continued in this capacity until 2011. It is seen here in a very short formation, between two Direct Rail Services Class 37s, at Darlington on 6 July 2008. The majority of vehicles in the No. 999xxx number series are purpose-built.

No. 999550, Darlington, 24 July 2006

The only purpose-built Mk 2 in departmental service is No. 999550, named the 'High Speed Track Recording Coach'. It operated locomotive-hauled test trains until it became part of the New Measurement Train in 2003. Replaced by a converted Mk 3, it returned to use in locomotive-hauled test trains. It is seen here in a formation powered by Class 37s at Darlington on 24 July 2006, still carrying the two long blue stripes from its time in the NMT.

No. 999550, Darlington, 23 August 2014

Some years later, No. 999550 received a repaint and lost the NMT blue stripes. Still in use as a track recording coach, it is seen at Darlington on 23 August 2014.

No. 62287, Darlington, 30 May 2016

In 2016, Network Rail began to brand their test trains, identifying each vehicle's function along with the words 'Improving Your Railway' to increase public awareness of their operations. Here No. 62287, a former Class 421 Motor Brake Standard, bears the wording 'Ultrasonic Test Unit' when seen at Darlington on 30 May 2016. EMU motor coaches were favoured for the UTU trains due to their bogie frames; as they were designed to carry traction motors, they were ideal for supporting the weight of ultrasonic test equipment.

No. 999602, Doncaster, 13 November 2008

The only Class 432 vehicles still in existence both went on to enter departmental service after withdrawal. No. 999602 is converted from Driving Motor Brake No. 62483 of set No. 3015/2015. The heavy bogies, with frames designed to support the weight of the Class 432's powerful traction motors, were ideal candidates for Ultrasonic Test Train coaches. No. 999602 operated within a converted Class 101 for a number of years before conversion to a locomotive-hauled coach. Other than the bogies, there is little to suggest No. 999602 was ever an EMU driving vehicle when it was seen at Doncaster on 13 November 2008. This is one of a small handful of No. 999xxx vehicles that aren't purpose-built.

No. 999606, Doncaster, 28 March 2012

While the No. 999xxx number series is usually used for purpose-built vehicles, two ultrasonic test coaches that were converted from Mk 1 EMU vehicles have found their way into that series. No. 999606 is one such vehicle, converted from Class 421 Motor Brake Standard No. 62356 (from unit No. 1850). As the test equipment is fitted to the bogies, Southern Region Mk 1 EMUs found favour thanks to their heavy-duty bogie underframes. With the motors removed, they were ideal for the ultrasonic test instruments. No. 999606 is seen in the formation of a test train at Doncaster West Yard on 28 March 2012.

No. 999606, Darlington, 27 May 2013

Ultrasonic Test Unit No. 999606 passes Darlington on 27 May 2013, far from its traditional stamping ground when it was a Class 421 motor coach.

No. 43013, Darlington, 13 October 2012

The New Measurement Train (NMT) was introduced in May 2003, using ex-Virgin CrossCountry power cars No. 43013, No. 43014 and No. 43062 and a selection of Mk 3 and Mk 2F coaches. Capable of 125 mph, the NMT is a common sight throughout the country where it is used to measure tracks and overhead wires, though shortly after introduction the Mk 2F coaches were replaced with much more suitable Mk 3s. The older coaches were reported to give a very lively ride at speeds above 100 mph!

No. 43062, Darlington, 23 January 2017

Illuminated by the early morning winter sun, No. 43062 *John Armitt* approaches a signal check at Darlington with a Heaton–Derby working on 23 January 2017. Of the three NMT power cars, this is the only one not fitted with buffers and drawgear on the outer end.

No. 43014, Stockton, 1 August 2011

Lacking lining and Network Rail logos, a very plain No. 43014 leads the New Measurement Train into Stockton on 1 August 2011 with a working to Derby via the Durham coast. It is leading an unusually short formation, with only four test train coaches instead of the usual five.

No. 43014, York, 31 May 2008

A weathered No. 43014 waits for a path north at York's Platform 10 on 31 May 2008, with what was at the time a regular Saturday morning working to Heaton Traction and Rolling Stock Maintenance Depot (T&RSMD).

No. 43013, Darlington, 23 January 2017

Freshly rebranded with Network Rail's 'Improving Your Railway' branding, No. 43013 brings up the rear of a New Measurement Train formation at Darlington on 23 January 2017. The signal in the distance has just changed to green to allow the train to continue after waiting several minutes for a path. This power car bears a small plaque toward the inner end reading '40 Years 1976 | 2016', marking four continuous decades of HST operation.

No. 43062, Darlington, 12 July 2014

Class 43 No. 43062 *John Armitt* brings up the rear of the New Measurement Train at Darlington. Along with No. 43013 and No. 43014, it entered departmental service in 2003, having been withdrawn by Virgin CrossCountry the previous year.

No. 43062, Darlington, 31 May 2010

Bringing up the rear of the NMT at Darlington on 31 May 2010 is No. 43062. It was named *John Armitt* in recognition of Network Rail's former Chief Executive at a ceremony at London Euston in 2007.

No. 975814, Darlington, 23 January 2017

A coach with a long departmental history, No. 975814 was built as First Open No. 11000 in 1972 as part of the prototype HST formation. Renumbered 41000 when the set was reclassified as the unique Class 252, it was withdrawn from passenger service in 1977 and converted into 'Test Car 10'. It saw a lengthy career with high-speed testing for the APT and Classes 89–91. After withdrawal it spent time at Peak Rail, Darley Dale and Barrow Hill before being acquired by Network Rail. It returned to service in the New Measurement Train in 2003. It is seen here in the current Network Rail livery at Darlington on 23 January 2017.

No. 975984, Darlington, 12 July 2014

Originally built in 1972 as prototype Mk 3 buffet No. 11000, before being renumbered 40000, No. 975984 was used as Laboratory 15 *Argus* and Test Car 4. Falling out of use in the early 2000s, scrapping beckoned before the coach was chosen to be part of the New Measurement Train. Returning to service in 2003, No. 975984 has been a constant part of the NMT ever since, travelling the length and breadth of the UK. It is seen in a mixed NMT formation passing Darlington on 12 July 2014.

No. 975984, Darlington, 6 November 2015

Still carrying the original blue-stripe NMT livery, No. 975984 is seen at Darlington on 6 November 2015. It has since been repainted and carries Network Rail's current 'Improving Your Railway' branding.

No. 977984, Heaton, 14 September 2008

Originally entering service in 1976 as Unclassified Kitchen No. 40501 in No. 253001, No. 977984 was converted for the New Measurement Train in 2003. Acting as a generator/mess vehicle it doesn't carry any test equipment, but it has been a regular part of the NMT ever since it entered service. It is seen here at Heaton T&RSMD on 14 September 2008. Ventilation grilles for the generator are visible at the nearest end.

No. 977984, Carlisle, 27 April 2013

No. 977984's past career as a restaurant coach is clearly visible at Carlisle on 27 April 2013. This is the side of the coach where a side corridor took passengers past the kitchen area, identifiable by the half-height windows at the nearest end.

No. 977984, Darlington, 23 January 2017

Recently repainted No. 977984 carries the latest Network Rail 'Improving Your Railway' branding at Darlington on 23 January 2017.

No. 977993, Darlington, 2 September 2013

Converted from Mk 3 Trailer Guard Standard No. 44053 in 2004, No. 977993 was one of two coaches that replaced Mk 2Fs in the New Measurement Train shortly after it was introduced. Fitted with equipment to monitor overhead lines, it acts as a high-speed track recording coach in the current formation. It is seen in an NMT formation at Darlington on 2 September 2013.

No. 977993, Darlington, 21 May 2011

Carrying a pantograph, No. 977993 is in an NMT formation at Darlington on 21 May 2011. It is not clear if the pantograph was ever used and it has since been removed.

No. 977993, Darlington, 23 January 2017

Recently repainted track/overhead-line-monitoring coach No. 977993 pauses at Darlington on a Heaton–Derby working on a bright January morning.

No. 977994, York, 31 May 2008

The second of two Mk 3s added to the NMT to replace older Mk 2Fs, No. 977994 was converted from surplus Trailer Guard Standard No. 44087 in 2004. As with the other vehicles in the NMT, it received two thin blue stripes below the windows to break up the all-over yellow. It is seen leaving York on 31 May 2008.

No. 977994, Carlisle, 27 April 2013

Some years later, No. 977994 is in a weathered plain yellow livery when it was captured at Carlisle on 27 April 2013.

No. 977994, Darlington, 23 January 2017

Along with the rest of the NMT, No. 977994 received a fresh coat of yellow and Network Rail's contemporary 'Improving Your Railway' branding, along with prominent 'New Measurement Train' branding. It is still considered 'new' despite fourteen years of service! Early morning winter sun catches the new branding at Darlington on 23 January 2017.

No. 977995, Darlington, 6 November 2015

No. 977995, former HST buffet No. 40619, was added to the New Measurement Train in 2005. A high-speed track recording, it is seen more occasionally in NMT formations. It is seen here at Darlington on 6 November 2015.

No. 977996, Heaton, 14 September 2008

Mk 3 Trailer Guard Standard No. 44062 enjoyed a short departmental career between 2007 and 2008 as part of the 'Hayabusa' project. Fitted with batteries, it worked with HST power car No. 43089 as part of the New Measurement Train. A joint venture between Network Rail, Hitachi, Brush Traction and Porterbrook Leasing, the power car relied on batteries to start, with the existing diesel engine taking over as the train reaches 30 km/h. The batteries were charged using regenerative braking. Designed to reduce fuel consumption, the trial lasted until October 2008. This coach is now based at the Leicestershire offices of Bachmann Model Railways.

New Measurement Train, Darlington, 12 July 2014

During the summer of 2014, most of the New Measurement Train's Mk 3 coaches were undergoing overhauls at Derby. During this time, the NMT power cars were used with a variety of Mk 1, 2 and 3 coaches. This very mixed formation is seen at Darlington heading to Heaton on 12 July 2014.

No. 45112, NMT, Darlington, 9 September 2003

A contender for 'working of the year' occurred on 9 September 2003 when the New Measurement Train failed at Heaton with a broken speedometer. Merlin Rail were contracted to drag the train to Derby for repairs, for which Fragonset's No. 45112 *The Royal Army Ordnance Corps* (the only mainline-certified Class 45 during the privatised era) was employed, travelling from Derby early that morning. The 'Peak' is seen here passing Darlington while taking the NMT home.

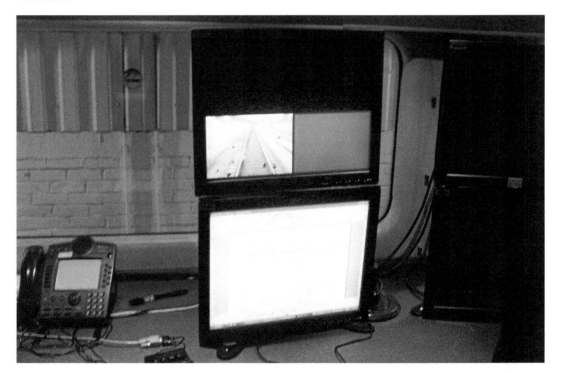

NMT Interior (1), Heaton, 14 September 2008

The NMT's wide array of instruments are fed to monitors on board the advanced test train. The upper monitor shows a view from the cab-mounted camera fitted to No. 43062. As the other power car, No. 43089, was not fitted with a forward camera, the other half of the screen is blank.

NMT Interior (2), Heaton, 14 September 2008

Rack-mounted equipment installed in one of the NMT's monitoring coaches. Labelled 'Image processor', they are designed to monitor the stream of images from the NMT's many external cameras and report possible defects to staff working on the train.

NMT Interior (3), Heaton, 14 September 2008

Another workstation on the New Measurement Train, this time showing general information on the train itself.

NMT Interior (4), Heaton, 14 September 2008
A bogie-mounted camera gives an onboard NMT operator a close-up view of the track.

NMT Interior (5), Heaton, 14 September 2008
A roof-mounted camera on No. 977993 is relayed to a screen for an operator to review. This is used to measure the position and condition of overhead wires. Unlike Overhead Line Monitoring Coach No. 975091, the roof-mounted equipment isn't in contact with the lines.

No. 37419, No. 975025, Darlington, 21 September 2016

Direct Rail Service operate the inspection saloon No. 975025 *Caroline* (a former Class 203 buffet car converted in 1969) on behalf of Network Rail, a duty usually placed in the hands of a Class 37/4. Taking a break from passenger duties, No. 37419 propels the saloon through Darlington on 21 September 2016.

No. 975025, Doncaster, 3 June 2010

Carrying a large number of railway staff, No. 975025 is propelled into Doncaster by Direct Rail Services' No. 37423 on the evening of 3 June 2010. From this angle, the vehicle's narrow body can be seen as the vehicle was built to the Southern Region's 'Hastings' loading gauge.

No. 975025, Derby, 13 September 2014

Caroline was one of a number of departmental visitors to the Derby Etches Park open day on 13 September 2014. As part of this vehicle's notable history, in 1992 it formed the first passenger train to venture into the Channel Tunnel – albeit for just a few hundred metres!

No. 950001, Darlington, 13 March 2014

A unique item in Network Rail's fleet is No. 950001. A purpose-built DMU based on the Class 150/1 design, it was built in York in 1987. Originally designated Class 180, it later became the sole example of Class 950. Designed as a track recording unit, it can be seen all over the national network. It is seen here leaving Darlington for a trip to Bishop Auckland and back on the morning of 13 March 2014. It is now the only departmental DMU left in service.

No. 950001, Peterborough, 24 March 2013
No. 950001 leaves a snowy Peterborough on 24 March 2013 on a lengthy trip around the Midlands.

No. 901001, Derby, 4 September 2005
Converted from a pair of Class 101 Driving Motor Brake Standards, No. 901001 consisted of No. 977391 (previously No. 51433) and No. 977392 (previously No. 53167). Used with No. 999602, they formed an ultrasonic test unit, being one of two departmental Class 101s that outlived the rest of the class by some years. Eventually withdrawn in 2007, No. 901001 was stored at Derby's RTC before entering preservation at the Churnet Valley Railway, where it was eventually scrapped in May 2012. Uniquely, for a first generation DMU, it was fitted with air brakes in order to work with No. 999602, which also allowed it to work with other coaching stock when needed.

No. 960010, Aylesbury, 6 July 2007

Sandite unit No. 960010 (consisting of No. 977858) is one of many Class 121s converted to departmental use. Painted in lined BR maroon, it was owned and used by Chiltern Railways. Withdrawn in 2004, it spent a long period in store alongside Aylesbury station before moving to Tyseley in 2011. It is now preserved at the Chinnor & Princes Risborough Railway.

No. 960011, Darlington, 11 September 2003

Former Class 121 55025 enjoyed a varied departmental career between 1993 and 2007. Originally a sandite unit, it then became a track survey unit for Railtrack and Balfour Beatty. It later became a route learner, receiving a fresh application of obsolete Railtrack blue/green in 2006. It was sidelined in October 2007 with wheelset issues just weeks before intended withdrawal. It is now preserved and in storage at Long Marston awaiting a long-term home.

No. 960013, Aylesbury, 6 July 2007

Over a decade into privatisation, Network SouthEast livery remains on sandite unit No. 960013. Last thought to have seen use in 2003, it is seen at Aylesbury on 6 July 2007. It was scrapped at the nearby depot in April 2011 after spending years yielding spare parts for Chiltern's operational Class 121s.

No. 960014, Aylesbury, 6 July 2007

Initially a sandite unit, No. 960014 was repainted in British Rail blue/grey livery in early 2000s when it became a route learner with Chiltern Railways. It was hired out to other operators on occasion, including sister company Wrexham, Shropshire & Marylebone Railway. This vehicle moved to Southall in 2016, where it is now stored.

No. 960013, No. 960014, Aylesbury, 6 July 2007

Former Class 121s No. 960013 and No. 960014 – the former being in storage while the latter was still part of Chiltern Railway's working fleet – rest alongside Aylesbury station on 6 July 2007. At the time this siding was a good vantage point for seeing the Class 117, 121 and 122 DMUs in Chiltern Railways' ownership.

No. 960015, Aylesbury, 6 July 2007

Once the last Class 122 in mainline use, No. 960015 was used as a sandite unit. It is seen here in Network Rail yellow livery at Aylesbury on 6 July 2007. Built in 1958, it was converted to departmental use as a sandite and route learning unit in 1970. Last used in the summer of 2004, it is now owned by the Llanelli & Mynydd Mawr Railway who plan to return it to passenger use.

No. 960021, Aylesbury, 6 July 2007

One of a handful of vehicles painted in a grey/white/dark orange livery adopted by Railtrack, No. 977723 (set number No. 960021) was converted from Class 121 No. 55021. Used as both a sandite and route learning unit, it was last thought to have been used around 2001. It joined a number of serviceable and unserviceable units on a siding adjacent to Aylesbury station, where it was seen on 6 July 2007. A source of spare parts for Chiltern's Class 121s, it was cut up at the nearby depot in April 2011.

No. 960301, Aylesbury, 6 July 2007

The last Class 117 to operate on the national network was No. 960301, a water cannon unit owned and operated by Chiltern Railways. Painted in British Rail green, the unit was originally a two-car formation before a third vehicle was added. Now withdrawn, the unit could often be seen in a long formation of departmental vehicles that belonged to Chiltern Railways alongside Aylesbury station, where it is seen on 6 July 2007.

No. 977992, Aylesbury, 6 July 2007

The third vehicle added to No. 960301 was No. 977992. Converted from Class 117 Driving Motor Standard No. 51375, this vehicle is unique in being a driving vehicle that was converted into an intermediate vehicle. The cab was replaced with the corridor end of another vehicle. After withdrawal, it moved to the Chinnor & Princes Risborough Railway in 2015.

No. 999801, Nuneaton, 5 July 2007

Resembling on-track plant more than a departmental unit, No. 999801 is a survey car built by Plasser in 2004. Along with sister vehicle No. 999800, it is used to measure track geometry and ballast depth. It is pictured here between duties at Nuneaton on 5 July 2007.

No. 6354 and No. 6352, Doncaster, 2 September 2005

Among the small handful of departmental vehicles to see use with passenger TOCs are barrier coaches No. 6352 and No. 6354. Converted from Mk 2 coaches, they were fitted with tightlock couplers at one end to allow Mk 4 coaches to be moved outside of a normal full set. Painted in GNER's blue/red livery, they are parked alongside a Class 91 in Doncaster's West Yard on 2 September 2005.

No. 6353, York, 2 June 2012

Mk 2A barrier coach No. 6353 (previously First Corridor No. 13478/19478) was still wearing the livery of long-defunct operator GNER when it was photographed at York on 2 June 2012. By this time it was used by nationalised operator East Coast. Fitted with a tightlock coupler at one end, it is used when Mk 4 coaches require moving outside of their fixed sets.

No. 6330, Crewe, 19 July 2014

Vehicles with certain types of coupler require 'barrier coaches' when a locomotive cannot be directly coupled to them. Converted from former passenger coaches, these vehicles are typically employed on stock moves between depots and works. Converted from Mk 2A Brake First Corridor No. 14084, No. 6330 (previously No. 975629) is used with HST trailers. It is seen here at Crewe, utilised to move a set of First Great Western Mk 3s to Kilmarnock for conversion work on 19 July 2014.

No. 6338, Crewe, 19 July 2014

Previously a Mk 1 gangwayed brake, No. 6338 is a barrier vehicle used by GWR for HST stock moves. Painted in plain First Great Western blue, it is seen at Crewe on 19 July 2014 conveying Mk 3 Trailer Firsts to Kilmarnock for conversion to standard class coaches.

No. 6356, Barrow Hill, 13 August 2006

Converted from Mk 2C No. 9455, No. 6356 is a Mk 4 barrier coach. Fitted with tightlock couplers at one end, it was withdrawn in the early years of privatisation. It is seen in storage at Barrow Hill on 13 August 2006. It was later moved to the Mid-Norfolk Railway before being scrapped at CF Booth, Rotherham, in November 2009.

No. 6357, Barrow Hill, 13 August 2006

Similarly modified to No. 6356, No. 6357 was another Mk 4 barrier vehicle, also a Mk 2C Brake Standard Open. It was seen alongside No. 6356 at Barrow Hill on 13 August 2006. After a time at the Mid-Norfolk Railway it was scrapped at CF Booth in May 2012.

No. 6392, Darlington, 3 April 2010

Mk 1 barrier coach No. 6392 (previously gangwayed brake No. 81588/92183) passes Darlington on a stock move on 3 April 2010, conveying a Grand Central HST trailer.

No. 6397, Darlington, 3 April 2010

Another barrier coach, No. 6397 (previously gangwayed brake No. 81600/92190) brings up the rear of a stock move at Darlington on 3 April 2010. While it is not bridging two vehicles with incompatible couplers, barrier vehicles are normally carried on the rear of stock moves to facilitate easier shunting, or rescues should the locomotive fail.

No. 6399, Derby, 4 September 2005

Based at Derby Etches Park, Midland Mainline's No. 6399 was an HST barrier coach that was used when Mk 3 coaches (with buckeye couplers) require shunting. Converted from Mk 1 gangwayed brake No. 92994, evidence of the plated-over doors and windows can be seen.

No. 975974, Doncaster, 28 March 2012

Wearing the distinctive livery of Arlington Fleet Services, Mk 1 barrier coach (former restaurant coach 1030) No. 975974 *Paschar* is used to move EMUs fitted with tightlock couplers. It is seen behind the fence at Wabtec's Doncaster Works on 28 March 2012.

No. 975978, Doncaster, 28 March 2012

Partnered with No. 975974 is No. 975978 *Perpetiel*, also owned by Eastleigh-based Arlington Fleet Services. The two barrier coaches are usually kept as a pair, known as 'Set T5'. On 28 March 2012, it was noted at Doncaster coupled to No. 975974.

No. 975976, Eastleigh Works, 24 May 2009

EMU barrier coach No. 975976 is still wearing the long-obsolete livery of Network SouthEast when it was photographed at Eastleigh works on 24 May 2009. Out of use for a number of years, it was broken up in January of the following year.

No. 9488, Darlington, 9 August 2010

A former First Great Western brake coach that saw quasi-departmental use was No. 9488. After a period in store following withdrawal from passenger use in 2006, it was used by Grand Central as a barrier vehicle for HST stock moves. Removed at Darlington with wheelset problems, No. 9488 spent more than a year in a siding, where it is seen on 9 August 2010 with graffiti damage dating from the earlier period in storage. It later moved to Heaton for use as a barrier vehicle within the depot only. Later sold to Direct Rail Services, it has now been returned to use on passenger services with ScotRail.

No. 5710, Heaton, 14 September 2008

Still wearing the earlier livery of First Great Western, Mk 2D Standard Open No. 5710 is in use as a barrier vehicle at Heaton T&RSMD. This particular vehicle was used solely within the confines of the depot for shunting Grand Central Mk 3 coaching stock.

No. 9428, Carlisle Kingmoor, 18 July 2015

One of two coaches used as nuclear escort vehicles, No. 9428 is a Mk 2A Brake Standard Open owned and operated by Direct Rail Services. The coaches are typically used when DRS are moving spent nuclear fuel rods on behalf of the Ministry of Defence, carrying guards for this high-security traffic. The public were given a chance to get a closer look at this coach on 18 July 2015 when it was on display at an open day at Carlisle Kingmoor.

No. 9419, Crewe Gresty Bridge, 19 July 2014

The second of two such coaches in DRS ownership, No. 9419 is on display at Direct Rail Services' Crewe Gresty Bridge depot during an open day on 19 July 2014. Due to the sensitive nature of their use, the modifications made to the coaches are largely unknown, but the most visible alteration is the removal of the corridor connection at each end, being replaced instead with a window to give the on-board escorts a view of their cargo. The MoD flask wagon is usually marshalled between the two coaches.

No. 6310 (No. 975325), Darlington, 29 August 2016

Some departmental coaches see use outside what would be considered 'special' use. Generator van No. 6310, owned by Riviera Trains, is used to provide power for coaching stock in charter trains where the locomotives may not be equipped with Electric Train Supply (ETS). No. 6310 was previously numbered No. 975325 by British Rail, where it supplied 415 V three-phase ETS to HST trailer sets hauled by conventional diesel locomotives.

No. 975554, Doncaster, 3 July 2005

Under British Rail, a large number of coaches were converted for the installation and maintenance of overhead wires. Mk 1s were often used for these conversions, which involved adding a flat roof for access to wires. After the East Coast Main Line electrification was completed in 1991, use of these coaches declined and today road/rail vehicles and self-propelled Multi-Purpose Vehicles are utilised instead.

No. 975555, Doncaster, 3 July 2005

Converted from Mk 1 Brake Standard Corridor 35164, No. 975555 was an office and staff coach in Overhead Line Maintenance (OHLM) use. Withdrawn by the 1990s, it spent a long period out of use at Doncaster West Yard before disposal at CF Booth in July 2007.

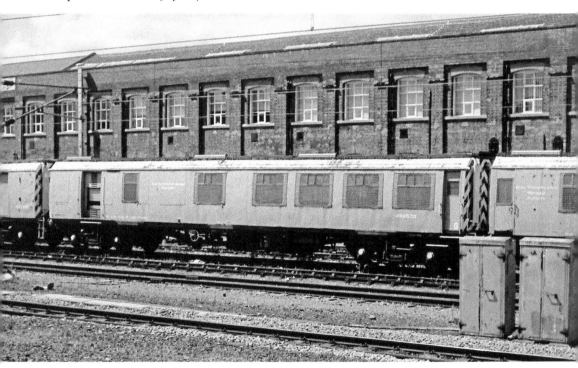

No. 975721, Doncaster, 3 July 2005

A generator and stores coach converted from Mk 1 Standard Corridor No. 25600, No. 975721 was another OHLM coach left in Doncaster West Yard for a number of years. Like No. 975554 and No. 975555, it was cut up at CF Booth in July 2007.

No. 977084, Barrow Hill, 13 August 2006

Many locomotive works around the country used to have their own test trains, a set of coaches intended to provide a load for newly overhauled locomotives to haul on their initial test runs before being released for traffic. No. 977084 (former restaurant kitchen No. 1505) was one such coach, based at Crewe Works. Thought to have fallen out of use around 2000/2001, No. 977084 has spent time at Barrow Hill (for asbestos removal) and the Battlefield Line, where it currently resides.

No. 31105, Doncaster, 28 March 2012

Class 31 locomotives have a long association with test trains, dating back to No. 97203 and No. 97204/31970 in the 1980s. Since privatisation, Network Rail has owned a handful of Brush Type 2 locomotives for test train use, with the last example being withdrawn in 2017. No. 31105, Network Rail's oldest Class 31, rests in Doncaster West Yard on 28 March 2012.

No. 31105, Darlington, 17 April 2006

Class 31 No. 31105, at the time one of the oldest working diesel locomotives on the national network, leads a test train at Darlington. This locomotive is now stored.

No. 31105, Derby, 13 September 2014

Class 31 No. 31105 engages in shunting at Derby on 13 September 2014. Coupled to GBRf's No. 73119, it is shunting a test train formation at the former Railway Technical Centre (RTC), now the base of operations for Network Rail's fleet. By this time, the veteran locomotive was largely limited to shunting at the RTC.

No. 31106, Darlington, 27 May 2013

Alongside their own fleet, Network Rail used to hire in Class 31s from elsewhere. Privately owned Class 31 No. 31106, painted in British Rail blue, leads a short test train into Darlington on 27 May 2013. At the time of writing this locomotive has been out of use (beyond shunting at Derby) for several years, but is still regarded as mainline-registered.

No. 31233, Derby, 13 September 2014

The extra spotlights fitted to No. 31233 can be seen in this view at Derby on 13 September 2014. It and No. 31285 were fitted with these lights at one end only.

No. 31285, Darlington, 19 August 2005

Network Rail's No. 31285 passes Darlington on a light engine move on 19 August 2005. This locomotive is now owned by HNRC, awaiting future developments for a possible return to traffic.

No. 31459, Darlington, 20 March 2009

At the time, No. 31459 was owned by Rail Vehicle Engineering Ltd (now part of Loram) when it was hired out to Serco Railtest for test train use. It is seen passing Darlington on 20 March 2009 with a stock move, taking a New Measurement Train power from Heaton to Derby.

No. 31465, Darlington, 1 December 2010
No. 31465 brings up the rear of a test train at snow-bound Darlington on the morning of 1 December 2010.

No. 37025, Darlington, 30 May 2016
In 2016, the Scottish Thirty-Seven Group's mainline-registered No. 37025 (named *Inverness TMD*) was hired by Colas Rail Freight for test train duties. The immaculately kept locomotive is seen passing Darlington with an Ultrasonic Test Unit working on 30 May 2016. At the time of writing the locomotive is still on hire to Colas and is expected to remain with the operator until late 2017.

No. 37116, Darlington, 22 May 2016

Acquired from preservation, No. 37116 returned to service after a lengthy overhaul. The former *Sister Dora* is seen leading a test train through Darlington on 22 May 2016.

No. 37219, Doncaster, 7 April 2017

In order to reduce reliance on hired locomotives, Colas Rail Freight acquired a number of Class 37s for test train duties. One such locomotive is No. 37219, one of the first locomotives to return to use with the operator. Now bearing the name *Jonty Jarvis 8-12-1998 to 18-3-2005*, No. 37219 rests in Doncaster West Yard on 7 April 2017. Sister locomotive No. 37175 was on the other end of the formation.

No. 37219, Darlington, 4 March 2016

Breaking through the clouds, the sun glints off Colas Rail Freight's No. 37219's side and roof as it brings up the rear of a test train working at Darlington on 4 March 2016.

No. 37402 and SGT, Norwich, 22 March 2013

Direct Rail Services' No. 37402 rests at Norwich with the Structure Gauging Train (SGT) on 22 March 2013. This version of the SGT was withdrawn shortly afterward, replaced with a pair of Mk 2 coaches.

No. 37423, Darlington, 23 August 2014

Class 37 No. 37423 *Spirit of the Lakes*, wearing the latest Direct Rail Services' livery, propels a Plain Line Pattern Recognition and Track Recording train through Darlington on 23 August 2014.

No. 37604, No. 37601, Darlington, 2 April 2013

No. 37604 leads a varied formation for a stop at Darlington on 2 April 2013, with No. 37601 on the rear.

No. 37218, No. 977974, No. 5981, No. 37605, Darlington, 20 April 2013

No. 37218 (nearest) and No. 37605 power a short test train formation (consisting of No. 977974 and No. 5981) through Darlington on 20 April 2013.

No. 37421, Darlington, 2 April 2016

Colas Rail Freight's No. 37421 speeds south through Darlington on 2 April 2016. Despite hauling departmental stock, it was taking part in a test run for hired-in No. 37025, which was being cleared for 85 mph running in order to join Colas' departmental fleet.

No. 37604, Darlington, 2 April 2013

Direct Rail Services' No. 37604 is at the head of a DB Schenker-operated test train at Darlington on 2 April 2013, where it is awaiting a path north.

No. 37604, Newcastle, 23 January 2017

Some years later, Direct Rail Services-owned No. 37604 is still working test trains, albeit now being operated by Colas Rail Freight. The veteran English Electric locomotive leads a test train into Newcastle on 23 January 2017.

No. 37606, Darlington, 17 July 2014

In 2006, Direct Rail Services began providing locomotives for test trains operated by Serco Railtest. Initially, only Class 37/6s were used due to traction knowledge purposes, and years later these locomotives can still be found on test trains operated by Colas Rail Freight. Here, No. 37606 is seen passing Darlington on 17 July 2014.

No. 37608, Palmersville (Newcastle), 23 January 2017

Alongside their own Class 37 fleet, Colas Rail Freight often hire locomotives from other companies. Europhoenix are one such provider, and on 23 January 2017 No. 37608 *Andromeda* is seen passing Palmersville with a test train working to Blyth with Direct Rail Services' No. 37604 on the rear.

No. 97301, Darlington, 4 March 2016

Formerly No. 37100, No. 97301 is one of four Class 37s currently used by Network Rail. As they were reclassified as Class 97/3s, the old British Rail classification for departmental locomotives was brought back into use when these four Class 37s were returned to working order for trialling the European Rail Traffic Management System (ERTMS) in Wales. Initially used on the Cambrian route between Shrewsbury and Aberystwyth, the four locomotives can also see use on general test trains around the country.

No. 97302, Darlington, 21 May 2011

Converted from No. 37170, No. 97302 found itself on more general duties away from the Cambrian Line on 21 May 2011, when it was involved in a stock move from Heaton to Derby, seen here passing Darlington.

No. 97303, Derby, 13 September 2014

The ERTMS test equipment is clearly visible under No. 97303 (the former No. 37178), where a fuel tank was sacrificed to house the new hardware. The locomotive is on display at Derby Etches Park on 13 September 2014.

No. 97304, Barrow Hill, 9 August 2009

The last of the Class 37s to be converted to an ERTMS test locomotive, No. 97304 (formerly No. 37217) was on display during an open weekend at Barrow Hill Roundhouse on 9 August 2009, coupled to sister locomotive No. 97302.

No. 43062, No. 977993, No. 99666, No. 97302, Darlington, 21 May 2011

European Rail Traffic Management System trial locomotive No. 97302 passes Darlington with a stock movement from Heaton to Derby on 21 May 2011. New Measurement Train vehicles No. 43062 and No. 977993 had to be dragged by the former Class 37, using No. 99666 as a barrier coach due to the HST vehicles having fixed buckeye couplers.

No. 67023, No. 977989, No. 488307, Darlington, 20 April 2004

Without any locomotives of their own, Serco Railtest hired in traction from EWS and Fragonset Railways. Class 67 No. 67023 is seen at Darlington on 20 April 2004 with a set of test coaches still in Railtrack blue/green livery. Class 67s had only recently taken over this work from Class 47/7s and thirteen years later No. 67023 is still associated with test trains in a more dedicated capacity.

No. 67027, Newcastle, 27 March 2017

With certain test train workings requiring 100 mph traction, Colas Rail Freight took the surprising step of acquiring a pair of Class 67s from DB at the end of 2016. Both locomotives returned to service with their new owners in early 2017, and on 27 March No. 67027 leads a test train into Newcastle on a working to Derby.

No. 67023, Newcastle, 27 March 2017

Partnered with sister locomotive No. 67027, No. 67023 brings up the rear of a test train at Newcastle on 27 March 2017. In their first few weeks with Colas Rail Freight, the two Class 67s covered a large part of the country, and are seen here travelling from Heaton to Derby (via Scotland!).

No. 68004, York, 27 March 2016

Prior to acquiring Class 67s, Colas Rail Freight took to subcontracting the operation of 100 mph test trains to Direct Rail Services, who used their flagship Class 68 locomotives. On 27 March 2016, No. 68004 *Rapid* leaves York with a northbound test train. No. 68016 was bringing up the rear.

No. 68016, Darlington, 12 January 2016

With No. 975091's pantograph raised, Direct Rail Services' No. 68016 *Fearless* heads a test train at Darlington on 12 January 2016. The need to test overhead wires at 100 mph on this occasion necessitated subcontracting this working to DRS. Colas Rail Freight now operate these trains in-house using Class 67s.

No. 86901 and No. 86902, York, 30 December 2008

Network Rail acquired Class 86 locomotives No. 86253, No. 86210 and No. 86424 in 2004 for conversion to mobile load banks. The first two were converted, becoming No. 86901 and No. 86902, while No. 86424 was retained for spare parts. Designed to draw current from overhead wires, the locomotives actually saw very little (if any) use in this capacity. Instead, they were employed on ice-clearing duties on the East Coast Main Line during winter months, usually being based at York while operated by Freightliner or Direct Rail Services. Both locomotives are seen at York on 30 December 2008.

No. 86901, York, 23 January 2009

Network Rail's No. 86901 is seen at York on 23 January 2009. With sister locomotive No. 86902, it usually ran back and forth between Newcastle and Hitchin during the early hours of the winter months, preventing hazardous build-ups of ice on overhead wires. This locomotive is now withdrawn, currently residing at the Rotherham scrapyard of CF Booth.

No. 86902, York, 9 March 2008

Usually partnered with No. 86901, No. 86902 is alone when seen here at York on 9 March 2008. After spending several winters on ice-clearing duties, both Class 86/9s fell out of use and were eventually withdrawn. After a long period languishing at CF Booth, Rotherham, the locomotive was finally cut up in late 2016.

No. BL2, Gosforth, 7 August 2005

The Tyne & Wear Metro utilises a fleet of three 1,500 V DC battery-electric locomotives, built by Hunslet in 1988. Numbered BL1 to BL3, they are used on engineering trains and the autumn Railhead Treatment Train (RHTT). They are also registered as Class 97s, numbered 97901–97903 for occasions when they need to work on Network Rail-owned infrastructure between Pelaw Junction and Sunderland. No. BL2 (No. 97902) is pictured here at Metro's Gosforth depot on 7 August 2005.

No. 041379, York, 27 April 2013

Former LMS Covered Carriage Truck (CCT) No. 35527, later tool van No. 395951, became a long-term resident of York Leeman Road Civil Engineers' depot as Internal User (IU) No. 041379. IU vehicles are those allocated to a specific purpose at a railway site, the intention being that they will only be moved internally within that site. A wide variety of IU vehicles existed at one point, though their numbers have dwindled in recent years. No. 041379 was used to store tools at the depot until 2015, when the body was scrapped. The underframe was moved to the Tanfield Railway for further use.

No. 042188, York, 27 March 2016

Mk 1 General Utility Van No. 93831 became an Internal User vehicle at York Works, gaining the number 042188. It was used to store Track Circuit Assister (TCA) parts. It was fitted with a small office with heating and lighting and was used to store TCA parts when the Class 165 DMUs were built in the early 1990s. Since the mid-1990s No. 042188 has resided at the nearby National Railway Museum and for many years was visible from passing trains north of York station.

No. 042236, Peterborough. 6 September 2005

Originally built as a humble 12-ton ventilated van, No. 778331 became No. 042236, an internal user stores van at Peterborough. Though it has moved around in recent years due to redevelopment of the extensive network of sidings north of Peterborough station, it remains a long-term resident of Spital sidings, often visible from passing trains.

No. DW139, York, 6 October 2010

Numbered in the ex-GWR departmental series for its entire working life, right up until the end of the 1980s, track-recording coach No. DW139 was a long-time resident at the National Railway Museum until moving to Barry Island in the summer of 2011. Seen here in October of the previous year, the coach was tucked out of the way in a siding in faded BR blue and grey livery.

No. 07007 (No. D2991), Eastleigh Works, 24 May 2009

No. 07007 enjoyed a lengthy departmental career at Eastleigh works as a mobile generator, numbered D2991 and still painted in BR green. After acquisition by Arlington Fleet Services, it was restored to working order and painted in BR blue. It gained the number 07007, which it never carried in BR service, and is now a working shunter at the Hampshire works.

No. 07007 (No. D2991) (2), Eastleigh Works, 24 May 2009

Enjoying the sun at Eastleigh Works, former static generator No. D2991 later returned to use as a working shunter and is on display at the works on 24 May 2009 during an open weekend.

No. 21661 (No. 902179), Grosmont, 5 May 2013

One of the oldest departmental vehicles in existence is No. 21661, originally built as a six-wheel third-class coach for the Stockton & Darlington Railway (as a subsidiary of the North Eastern Railway) in 1871. It became an inspection saloon in 1884 and was rebuilt with bogies twenty years later. It was finally withdrawn (as No. DE902179) in 1969, entering preservation at the Keighley & Worth Valley Railway. It is seen at Grosmont, on the North Yorkshire Moors Railway, on 5 May 2013 on a visit away from its home line.

No. 45053, York, 6 October 2010

Mobile Test Unit No. 45053 was a purpose-built departmental coach built by the LMS in 1938, designed for testing steam locomotives as part of the Mobile Test Plant with No. 45054, No. 45055 and No. 45059. They were later used to test other traction, remaining in service until 1976. Entering preservation, No. 45053 deteriorated during many years outside, including a lengthy period at the National Railway Museum. In 2011 it moved from York to the Embsay & Bolton Abbey Steam Railway for restoration.

No. 45053, York, 23 January 2009
A closer look at No. 45053 at York reveals the later 'Brake Unit 1' branding it received.

No. 45053, York, 23 January 2009
The condition of No. 45053's bodywork is all too apparent in this view at York on 23 January 2009.

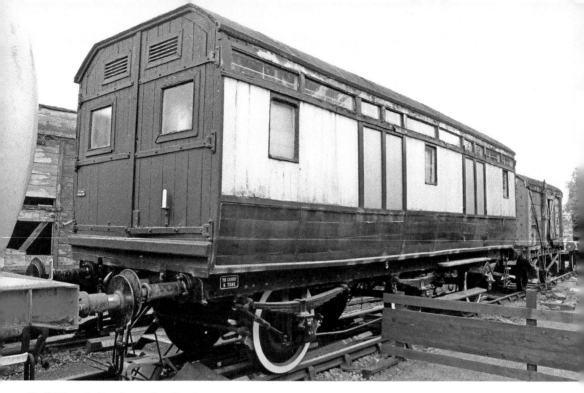

No. DM395361, Peterborough, 5 October 2013

Built in 1920, an LNWR Covered Carriage Truck would later become LMS motor car van No. 36993 then No. DM395361 for use by contractors at Henry Pooley & Son Ltd, who built and maintained weighing machines used in the railway industry. After withdrawal the coach was preserved at Peterborough and currently resides at the former Railworld site, now part of the Nene Valley Railway. Painted in LNWR livery, it is seen here on 5 October 2013.

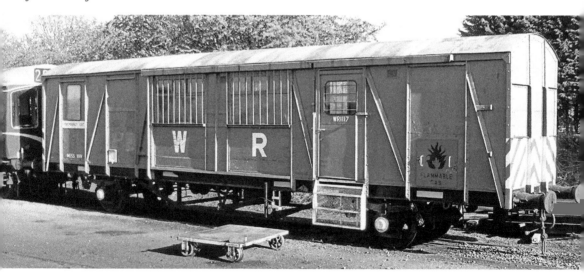

No. 786968, Leeming Bar, 10 April 2011

Originally built as a ferry van, No. 786968 later saw use as a civil engineer's mess van. After withdrawal the coach was preserved at the Wensleydale Railway and can usually be found at Leeming Bar. It still sees use as an engineer's vehicle in preservation, but has carried passengers on at least one occasion. Wearing a plain grey livery, it is seen in the small yard at Leeming Bar on 10 April 2011 carrying the number WR1117.

No. 902502, York, 2 June 2012

A historically important vehicle in the National Collection is No. 902502, a former NER/LNER dynamometer car. Dating from 1906, it is famous for the record-breaking run behind *Mallard* in 1938, when the world steam record was broken. Retired from service in 1951, it was saved for preservation and can usually be found at York's National Railway Museum, alongside the record-breaking A4 locomotive it is associated with.

No. 975874, Leeming Bar, 7 June 2013

In the late 1970s, British Rail began to look at ways to reduce the running costs of branch lines. They built a prototype railbus, using British Leyland National Mk 1 bus parts on top of a powered four-wheel underframe. Intended for bus-style operation whereby the driver would sell tickets as passengers boarded, No. 975874 was the first of several prototypes jointly developed by British Rail and British Leyland. It was largely a development test bed, even travelling to the USA for trials in 1980. It paved the way for the Class 140–144 'Pacer' family of railbuses that have been a common sight on Britain's railways since the early 1980s. Eventually secured for preservation by the National Railway Museum, it is currently on loan to the Wensleydale Railway, where it is seen on 7 June 2013.

No. 977989, Leeming Bar, 19 June 2016

No. 977989 was converted from Mk 3A sleeper No. 10536 in the early 2000s and was used as crew accommodation for Jarvis Rail's 'slinger' track renewal train. It was only used for a short period, being sidelined by 2006. After a number of years in storage it was secured for preservation by the Wensleydale Railway and is now used as volunteer accommodation at Leeming Bar.

APT-E, Shildon, 19 May 2013

A unique test train in British Rail's fleet was the Advanced Passenger Train – Experimental (APT-E). Built at the Derby RTC between 1970 and 1972, this gas-turbine-powered set would go on to break the British railway speed record in 1975, achieving 152.3 mph. After extensive tests at Old Dalby and on the Midland & Great Western Main Lines it was retired to the National Railway Museum, travelling to York on 11 June 1976. After many years outside it faced an uncertain future until a group of volunteers came together to ensure this unique piece of railway history survived. With a brighter future, it moved to the NRM's new site at Shildon in 2004, where work has continued, including extensive internal work. It is pictured inside the museum building on 19 May 2013.

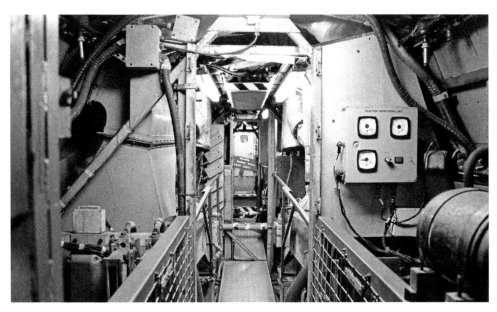

APT-E interor, Shildon, 24 May 2013

Each APT-E power car consists of five gas-turbine engines, with a sixth providing power for the coaches. This makes each power surprisingly spacious inside, with a central walkway connecting the cab to a rear door that gives access to the coaches. With interior lighting restored, the inside of one power car is well-illuminated during a look inside this unique train at the National Railway Museum, Shildon, on 24 May 2013.

APT-E interor, Shildon, 24 May 2013

The partially restored interior of the APT-E was opened to visitors on 24 May 2013, giving the public access to this unique train.

APT-E interor, Shildon, 24 May 2013

While British Rail removed much of the test equipment in APT-E when it was given to the National Railway Museum, Serco kindly donated a large quantity of old test instruments of a similar type and vintage to that originally fitted in the train, helping it to look the part. Much of this equipment is seem inside one of APT-E's trailer cars on 24 May 2013.

APT-E interor, Shildon, 24 May 2013

One of the APT-E's trailer cars featured a small VIP area, with seating for special guests. The restored VIP area was made accessible to visitors on 24 May 2013 at the Shildon branch of the National Railway Museum. Needless to say the flatscreen monitor on the wall is not an original feature, being added in preservation to show archive video footage of the APT's record-breaking test runs.

APT-E interor, Shildon, 24 May 2013

The APT-E's tilt equipment could be monitored and controlled from this workstation, with a control panel divided into four areas – one for each vehicle.

No. E1706E (No. DB975882), York, 27 March 2016

Built in 1948 to an LNER design, No. E1706E was a buffet car until 1978/79 when it became No. DB975882, a civil engineer's staff coach. It remained in this role until it was preserved at the Llangollen Railway, where it remains in use after being restored to its original form. It is seen here visiting the National Railway Museum, York, on 27 March 2016.

No. RB004, Shildon, 19 April 2009

With a Leyland-built body, No. RB004 was assembled at BREL Derby in 1984 and was used at the Mickleover test track as one of the final railbus development vehicles. Preserved in 1994, it now belongs to The Railbus Trust and is painted in a cream/brown livery similar to that carried by some Class 142s. Based at the Whitrope Heritage Centre, it carries passengers on the short preserved line. In 2009 it visited the National Railway Museum at Shildon, where it is seen taking part in their diesel gala on 19 April of that year.

No. 975672, York, 20 April 2014

During the 1970s and 1980s, large numbers of Southern Railway-designed four-wheel parcel and brake vans saw conversion to departmental use, with some surviving well into the 1990s. No. 975672 was converted from 1937-built 'Van C' No. 435 in the 1970s for use with single-buffer Southern Region EMU vehicles such as SUBs and EPBs. It was later preserved and became a long-term resident of the National Railway Museum's sidings close to York station. It was later sold to the Vale of Berkeley Railway, but it was seen here adjacent to the museum's car park on 20 April 2014.

No. 3058 (No. 975313), Scarborough, 25 August 2014

Converted into a HST instruction coach in the mid-1970s, No. 975313 left departmental service and entered preservation at the West Somerset Railway, becoming a buffet coach. It later returned to mainline service with West Coast Railway Company in 2011, having reverted to its previous identity of No. 3058.

No. 55012 (No. 977941), Shildon, 9 October 2011

Withdrawn by Regional Railways from Laira depot in January 1994, Class 122 No. 55012 later entered service with freight operator Loadhaul, as a route learning unit. It was renumbered No. 977941 but never carried that number. It was eventually stored and spent a long period left to the elements at Thornaby. Sold to preservation in 2009, by 2011 it had been restored to passenger-carrying condition and painted in BR green. It is seen at NRM Shildon on 9 October 2011 before moving to the Weardale Railway, where it is currently based.

No. 03179 (No. 97807), Wansford, 2 March 2008

Class 03 shunter No. 03179 entered departmental service in the late 1980s as a civil engineer's shunter on the Isle of Wight. With a cut-down cab roof it could fit on the island line's limited loading gauge, along with sister locomotive No. 03079. While it was assigned the departmental number 97807, it never carried it. Withdrawn in 1996, it was later returned to capital stock, becoming a working shunter at WAGN's depot in Hornsey, London. It has since entered preservation, but is seen here visiting the Nene Valley Railway on 2 March 2008 while in the ownership of WAGN's successor, First Capital Connect.

No. D5054/24054 (No. 968008), Barrow Hill, 19 April 2015

After withdrawal in August 1976, No. D5054/24054 entered departmental service as a train pre-heating unit on the Western Region. Renumbered No. 968008 and allocated to Newton Abbot, it was designed to keep rakes of coaches warm during the early morning, in a number series typically used for locomotives that could no longer run under their own power. It was finally retired in 1982 and secured to preservation. Restored to working order and painted in BR green livery, it is seen at Barrow Hill Roundhouse on 19 April 2015.

No. D5061 (No. 97201), Grosmont, 23 April 2004

As No. 968007, then No. 97201, No. D5061 went on to become the last Class 24 in British Rail's fleet, entering departmental service in 1976 as dedicated motive power for test trains. By 1979 it was renumbered 97201 and gained BR's departmental livery of blue/red with white lining. Later replaced by a Class 31 in 1987, it spent a long time in storage pending disposal, until it was finally preserved in 1991. Returned to BR green, it is now based at the North Yorkshire Moors Railway where it is seen on 23 April 2004.

No. 5 (No. 960900), Beamish, 8 September 2013

No. 5 is a Great Eastern Railway Royal Train coach that was converted to a manager's saloon, which saw use until 1972. After four decades out of use the coach was restored as a saloon and sees use at Beamish open-air museum, County Durham, where it is seen carrying passengers on 8 September 2013.